Juvenile

W9-BUU-563

The Funny Zone

SPORTS ZONE

Read Jokes. Write Jokes.

Jokes, Riddles, Tongue Twisters & "Daffynitions"

By Gary Chmielewski

Illustrated by Jim Caputo

SCHAUMBURG TOWNSHIP DISTRICT LIBRARY
JUVENILE DEPT.
130 SOUTH ROSELLE ROAD
SCHAUMBURG, ILLINOIS 60193

5108
apple

3 1257 01671 7281

A Note to Parents and Caregivers:

As the old saying goes, "Laughter is the best medicine." It's true for reading as well. Kids naturally love humor, so why not look to their interests to get them motivated to read? The Funny Zone series features books that include jokes, riddles, word plays, and tongue twisters-all of which are sure to delight your young reader.

We invite you to share this book with your child, taking turns to read aloud to one another, practicing timing, emphasis, and expression. You and your child can deliver the jokes in a natural voice, or have fun creating character voices and exaggerating funny words. Be sure to pause often to make sure your child understands the jokes. Talk about what you are reading and use this opportunity to explore new vocabulary words and ideas. Reading aloud can help your child build confidence in reading.

Along with being fun and motivating, humorous text involves higher order thinking skills that support comprehension. Jokes, riddles, and word plays require us to explore the creative use of language, develop word and sound recognition, and expand vocabulary.

At the end of the book there are activities to help your child develop writing skills. These activities tap your child's creativity by exploring numerous types of humor. Children who write materials based on the activities are encouraged to send them to Norwood House Press for publication on our website or future books. Please see page 24 for details.

Above all, the most important part of the reading experience is to have fun and enjoy it!

Sincerely,

793.735
CHMIELEWSKI, G

Shannon Cannon

Shannon Cannon
Literacy Consultant

NorwoodHouse Press

P.O. Box 316598 • Chicago, Illinois 60631
For information regarding Norwood House Press, please visit our website at: www.norwoodhousepress.com or call 866-565-2900.

Copyright © 2008 by Norwood House Press.
All rights reserved. No part of this book may be reproduced or utilized in any form or by any means without written permission from the publisher.

Designer: Design Lab
Project Management: Editorial Directions

Library of Congress Cataloging-in-Publication Data:
Chmielewski, Gary, 1946–
    The sports zone / by Gary Chmielewski; illustrated by Jim Caputo.
        p. cm. — (The funny zone series)
Summary: "Contains sports-themed jokes for children as well as exercises
to teach children how to write their own jokes"—Provided by publisher.
    ISBN-13: 978-1-59953-144-1 (library edition : alk. paper)
    ISBN-10: 1-59953-144-5 (library edition : alk. paper)
    1. Sports--Juvenile humor. I. Title.
PN6231.S65C44 2008
818'.5402—dc22
                                        2007016003

Printed in the United States of America

LET'S PLAY

What dogs watch stock car racing on TV?

Lap dogs!

Do you like soccer?

Yes, I get a kick out of it!

Where do bad gymnasts go?

Behind parallel bars!

Why can't Cinderella play soccer?

Her coach is a pumpkin!

Why can't you play any sports in the jungle?

Because of all the cheetahs!

3

Why didn't the nose make the volleyball team?
Nobody would pick him!

Little Kevin: "Mommy, I just found a lost ball."
Mother: "How do you know it was lost?"
Little Kevin: "The boy across the street is still looking for it."

Did you hear about the cheap boomerang?
You never get it back!

What do eggs and a losing team have in common?
They both get beaten!

Where do all the sports shirts come from?
Jersey!

What's the difference between a prizefighter and a man with a cold?
One knows his blows and the other blows his nose!

When is a boxer like an astronomer?

When he's seeing stars!

Why can't you always get a straight answer from a wrestler?

Sometimes they're hard to pin down!

What did one sports shoe say to the other?

Nothing – they were tongue-tied!

What are the three "R's" cheerleaders have to learn?

Rah! Rah! Rah!

Did you hear about the goofy athlete who won a gold medal at the Olympics?

He was so proud of it he had it bronzed!

5

Why did the cheerleading squad move into the haunted house?

It had spirit!

Laura: "Are you sure you've ridden a horse before?"

Rick: "Oh, yes."

Laura: "Then what kind of saddle would you like – with or without a horn?"

Rick: "I'll take the one without. I don't think I'll run into much traffic."

I used to be a ballet dancer but I decided it was *tutu* difficult.

Lisa: "I'm taking a course in parachute jumping."

Janine: "How many jumps do you have to make before you pass the course?"

Lisa: "All of them!"

A bicycle can't stand on its own because it is too *tired*.

Why is the stadium the coolest place?

All the fans are in the stands!

Stranger: "You catching any fish, kid?"

Tony: "Yes, sir! I caught at least 12 big ones."

Stranger: "Do you know who I am? I'm the local fishing warden."

Tony: "Do you know who I am? I'm the biggest liar in the county."

Why is bowling such a quiet game?

You can hear a pin drop!

What happens to old bowling balls?

They become marbles for elephants!

How did the archer get to the contest?

By following the arrows!

BATTER UP

What kind of socks do baseball players like?

Ones with lots of runs in them!

What is the biggest diamond in the world?

A baseball diamond!

Why do baseball players make such good friends?

They always go to bat for you!

What has 18 legs and catches flies?

A baseball team!

Rookie: "How do you hold a bat?"
Veteran: "By its wings!"

Does it take longer to run from first base to second base or from second base to third base?

Second base to third base because there is a shortstop!

EUROPE
What an umpire says
when it's your turn to bat!

Conor: "What does it take to hit a ball the way you do?"

Dalton: "A bat!"

Why were the baseball players hot and sweaty?

The fans went away!

SAFE!

What is the baseball player's favorite part of the playground?

The slide!

Marie: "My father taught his chickens to play baseball."

Darrell: "That must be fun to watch."

Marie: "Not really, they keep hitting fowl balls!"

In what part of the car do you keep your baseball mitt?

The glove compartment!

Umpire: "I have to admit, the players on your team are good losers."

Manager: "Good? They're perfect!"

Coach to the team: "You better start catching the fly balls or else I will put in some other players."

Team: "Gee, thanks! We can use the help!"

What monster goes to baseball games?

A double-header!

Did you hear about the softball team that won without ever putting a man on base?

It was an all-girl team!

Coach: "Sarah, what do you get when you reach third base?"

Sarah: "A triple."

Coach: "Right. What do you get when you hit the ball over the fence?"

Sarah: "A new ball!"

Thomas: "I'd like to return this baseball bat."

Salesman: "What's wrong with it?"

Thomas: "Every time I go to bat I strike out!"

Jade: "Did you hear the new song about baseball?

Lee: "No, why?"

Jade: "You should, it's a big hit!"

Why did the baseball player get arrested?

He was caught stealing bases!

Why did the campers bring a baseball player with them?

To pitch the tent!

Juan: "Do you really like baseball?"

Morgan: "Sure, don't you?"

Juan: "Not anymore."

Morgan: "Why not?"

Juan: "Every time I get to third base the coach yells at me to go home!"

HOOP-LA

Why are basketball players messy eaters?

They like to dribble!

What do baby basketballs do?

Dribble!

Why is a basketball player's hand never bigger than eleven inches?

Because 12 inches is a foot!

How do you cheer on a basketball player?

Hoop, Hoop, Hooray!

Fan: "I bet I can tell you the score of this game before it starts."

Ref: "Okay, smarty, tell me."

Fan: "Nothing to nothing!"

What happens when basketball players get sick?

Hooping Cough!

Alan: "Hey, coach, the doctor says I can't play basketball."

Coach: "I could have told you that."

13

TOUCHDOWN!

What football player wears the biggest helmet?

The one with the biggest head!

What do you call the football player who gives up?

The quitter-back!

What happens when a clumsy football player plays ball?

A field trip!

14

George: "What's the score of the game?"

Matt: "21 to 13."

George: "Who's winning?"

Matt: "21!"

Coach: "Remember all those blocking and tackling tips I gave you?"

Rookie: "I sure do."

Coach: "Well, forget them. We traded you!"

Did you hear about the person who got mad at the football game?
He thought "getting the quarterback" was a refund!

Coach: "Sandy, get in there."

Sandy: "But coach, I can't play football today. I sprained my ankle."

Coach: "That's a lame excuse!"

Did you hear about the college star fullback? He played with his team for seven years!

He could block and run – he just couldn't pass!

Why is an airline pilot like a running back?

They both want to make a touchdown!

Which professional football team has the largest players?

The New York GIANTS!

FORE!

Why is Tarzan banned from playing golf?

He screams with every swing!

Golfer: "Caddy, how would you have played that last shot?"

Caddy: "Under an assumed name."

Why did the golfer bring two pairs of pants to the game?

In case he got a hole in one!

Why is it so hard to drive a golf ball?

No steering wheel!

Why is bowling cheaper than playing golf?

No matter how badly you play, you never lose the ball!

Golfer In The Clubhouse: "Before I hire you, caddy, I need to know. Are you good at finding lost balls?"

Caddy: "Yes. I'm the best."

Golfer: "Good. You're hired. Now find some golf balls so we can start the game."

Golfer: "Any idea how I could cut about 10 strokes off my game?"

Caddy: "Yeah, quit on the sixteenth hole!"

First Golfer: "So, how's your game?"

Second Golfer: "I shoot in the 70's. But when it gets colder I quit."

How did they measure hail before golf balls were invented?

Gary: "Why don't you play golf with Brent anymore?"

Phillip: "Would you play with a cheat? Someone who moves the ball when you're not looking? Someone who writes down the wrong score?"

Gary: "Certainly not!"

Phillip: "Well, neither would Brent!"

ALL WET

Hannah: "Where did you learn to swim so fast?"

Kathryn: "In the water!"

How do monarchs swim?

They do the butterfly stroke!

Skin Diving

A mosquito's favorite sport!

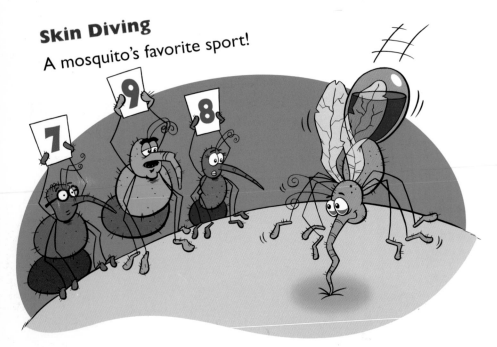

Christy: "We can't go swimming right now. We just ate. Mom said we shouldn't swim on a full stomach."

Danita: "Okay – we'll swim on our backs!"

How do swimmers get where they are going?

In car pools!

20

WHAT A RACKET!

What is a fly swatter's favorite sport?

Squash!

What can you serve but never eat?

A tennis ball!

Where do judges go to relax?

The tennis court!

Why are waiters and waitresses such good tennis players?

They know how to serve!

Why did the chicken run across the tennis court?

The referee called fowl!

What game did Godzilla play with people?

Squash!

Jimmy: "Can't you play tennis without making so much noise?"

Chris: "Don't be silly. You can't play without raising a racket!"

ON THE ICE

How do you kiss a hockey player?

You pucker up!

What position does the ghost play on the hockey team?

Ghoulie!

What color is a hockey score?

Goaled!

Which winter sport do you learn in the fall?

Ice-skating!

Mike: "Can you ice skate?"

Emily: "I don't know. I can't stand up long enough to find out!"

Why don't hockey players tell jokes on the ice?

The ice might crack up!

What did the hockey player ask the puck right before the game?

"Want to stick around for a while?"

RUN, RUN, RUN

What does the winner of the race lose?

His breath!

Did you hear about the track star that raced a rabbit?

He won by a hare!

Where do high jumpers store their valuables?

In a pole vault!

Allison: "Mom, can I join the track team?"
Mom: "Run that by me again?"

Why should everyone run?

We all belong to the human race!

What sport does a banana compete in?

Track and peeled!

Del: "Are you a runner yet?"
Lupita: "No, but I'm making great strides!"

What kind of sand do you run in to run faster?

Quicksand

What are two things a runner can't have for breakfast?

Lunch and dinner!

23

WRITING JOKES CAN BE AS MUCH FUN AS READING THEM!

A *pun* is a joke that uses words in funny ways. One way to make a pun would be to take two words that sound alike (or almost alike) but have different meanings. Next you switch the words, or make a *play on words*, to create the joke. It is important to remember that puns are very short, your audience must be familiar with the subject of your pun, and you get to the punch line quickly.

For example, the word *tired* can mean not having any energy or it can refer to the rubber *tires* on a bike. Also, *two* and *too* sound exactly alike. Here is the pun from page 6:

*A bicycle can't stand on its own because it is **too tired***.

Sometimes you can take a pun and make it into a riddle—a joke that is made up of a question and a funny answer. For example, here is the pun above made into a riddle:

Question: Why can't the bicycle stand on its own?

Answer: Because it's **too tired**.

Go back and re-read all the jokes in this book. Identify the jokes that are puns. Which ones do you think are funny? Think about why you think they are funny.

YOU TRY IT!

You can do this joke-writing exercise with a group of friends or by yourself. If you are in a group, divide up into two or three teams. Each team should pick a sport or favorite activity and write down words that come to mind when thinking about that sport or activity. It can be equipment, team names, or words used when playing the sport or doing the activity. Keep track of the time; try to stay within 10 minutes. Once you have listed all the sport's words, have each team say their words aloud. The entire group can then brainstorm and think up puns that go with the words. For example: if tennis was chosen as a sport, "racket" is probably on the list. Since racket has two meanings, it makes for a good pun: "I used to play tennis, but it just wasn't my racket." Write down as many jokes as you can come up with. Whether working in a group or by yourself, try the jokes out on other people. If they laugh, keep the joke. If they don't, either keep working on it or move on to another joke.

SEND US YOUR JOKES!

Pick out the best pun that you created and send it to us at Norwood House Press. We will publish it on our website — organized according to grade level, the state you live in, and your first name.

Selected jokes might also appear in a future special edition book *Kids Write in the Funny Zone*. If your joke is included in the book, you and your school will receive a free copy.

Here's how to send the jokes to Norwood House Press:

1) Go to www.norwoodhousepress.com.
2) Click on the **Enter the Funny Zone** tab.
3) Select and print the joke submission form.
4) Fill out the form, include your joke, and send to:
   The Funny Zone
   Norwood House Press
   PO Box 316598
   Chicago, IL 60631

Here's how to see your joke posted on the website:

1) Go to www.norwoodhousepress.com.
2) Click on the **Enter the Funny Zone** tab.
3) Select **Kids Write in the Funny Zone** tab.
4) Locate your grade level, then state, then first name.
   If it's not there yet check back again.